Loveology
God. Love. Marriage. Sex.
And the never-ending story of male and female.

John Mark Comer with Jay Fordice

We want to hear from you. Please send your comments about this
book to us in care of zreview@zondervan.com. Thank you.

ZONDERVAN

Loveology Study Guide
Copyright © 2014 by John Mark Comer

This title is also available as a Zondervan ebook.
Visit www.zondervan.com/ebooks.

Requests for information should be addressed to:
Zondervan, *Grand Rapids, Michigan 49530*

ISBN 978-0-310-68837-2

Cover design: Ryan Peterson
Interior production: Beth Shagene

Printed in the United States of America

HB 01.03.2024

Love-
ology

Study Guide

Contents

Introduction

The human race can take credit for a lot of things, but love isn't one of them.

Marriage and sexuality. Romance and dating. Masculinity and femininity. It was all part of God's creation. Marriage wasn't manufactured by society. Love wasn't designed by humans. It all came from God's brilliant imagination. Straight from his Genesis story.

We are the sons of Adam and the daughters of Eve. We carry the same DNA. We were designed for deep, meaningful, intimate relationships. We were set up to love. But somewhere along the way, just like Adam and Eve, we lost sight of what it all should look like.

Love is beautiful. It's hard and painful and arduous at times. But it is beautiful. And deep down, we know it is well worth the risk.

As you engage this five-week study, it is my hope that you will come to better understand what God intended back in the Garden. Before the forbidden fruit. Before the serpent. Before the fig leaves. If we can comprehend the brilliance behind God's original vision for love and marriage and sex and romance — if we can redefine that fuzzy, amorphous, confusing word "love" and look at it through the lens of Jesus — our marriages and relationships and lives will be reshaped from the ground up.

John Mark Comer

How to use this study

This is a five-week study on the theology of love based on the book *Loveology* by John Mark Comer. You can go through this study alone, but it was designed to be used for small groups and missional communities. The hope is you will get with people you know—those you do life with—and learn alongside each other. If you can, include individuals at different stages of life. Single people. Engaged couples. Those who have been married for a few years. You can learn a ton from those with a different vantage point.

Read the book together. Dig into the Scriptures. Watch the videos as a group. And explore what this all means for you. How will this redefinition change your dreams, your relationships, and your marriage—either now or in the future? Pray for one another. Challenge each other. Hold each other accountable.

Each session begins with a brief video from John Mark Comer highlighting the topic of the week. The video and discussion questions will correspond with specific chapters in the book. It is not necessary to read the book while you go through this study, but you are encouraged to do so. The reading will complement what you are learning, taking you deeper into vital content and helping you digest the key elements.

The rhythm for each week is simple. Read the intro for each session first. Get an understanding for the topic. Then watch the video. Following the video you will have time to discuss the questions provided in this study guide. There are a lot of questions. You don't have to cover all of them. Focus on the ones that most resonate with you and your group. Feel free to go back to the book or spend time digging into one of the Scripture references. Don't be afraid of the tough questions. Get your fingernails dirty. Scratch past the epidermis and explore the issues that really matter. You'll get what you put into this.

At the end of each session you will find a midweek study option for you to tackle on your own. These are optional, but highly recommended. If you have time, they will help you better understand the biblical basis for the teaching. After all, you shouldn't take John Mark's word for any of this. The only thing that matters is if you are in alignment with God.

Lastly, each session will end with the Scriptures and prayer. Nothing is more powerful than chewing on the Scriptures and letting them sink down deep into your core. Challenge yourself and your group to focus on memorizing these verses as you do the study.

You can find more insight for leaders at the end of this study guide.

12

Session 1

Love

Based on the preface and chapter 1 of the Loveology *book by John Mark Comer*

> Love is the source of our highest highs and lowest lows.
> Love is joy and laughter and gift and freedom and faith and
> healing, but when love goes south, it's a knife to the chest.

(*Loveology,* p.14)

Introduction • 2 minutes

If you know anything about the Gospels, you know people are always coming to Jesus with questions about anything and everything. They ask questions about life, God, theology, and law. You name it, they ask it.

In the book of Matthew, chapter 19, we read one example. The Pharisees—the religious teachers of the day—come to Jesus and test him. They ask him if it is lawful for a man to divorce his wife.

Contrary to what you might think, divorce was at pandemic levels in first-century Jewish culture. And sadly, more than 2,000 years later, here we are struggling with the same dysfunction and brokenness.

We are all facing abysmal odds when it comes to marriage and love. And many would argue it's because somewhere along the way we lost the plotline. We're confused, at best, when it comes to love.

Jesus answers the question of the Pharisees, but not in the way they expected. He points them back to the plotline—back to the beginning. It's from the lips of Jesus that we get our loveology.

Dig in • 3 minutes

Before you watch the video, take time to dig into the following question. Think about how it relates to you as an individual and then briefly discuss it as a group.

Just as in the first century, divorce is all around us. You'd be hard pressed to find anyone today not affected by divorce. How has divorce had an impact on you and your view of love and marriage?

Video • 10 minutes

Play the Session 1 video. Take notes as you watch. What resonates with you? What concepts or thoughts are new to you? What do you disagree with?

Video notes

Tension between the world and God

Fifty percent fail rate: Fear and insecurity regarding marriage

Jesus' view of divorce

The faulty view of "falling in love"

What is love?

Deep feelings of affection versus active involvement

Jesus' example

Rayah, *dod*, and *ahavah*

Group discussion • 40 minutes

First impressions

Take a minute as a group to talk about a few things that hit you from the video. Refer to your notes and share around the group.

Asking the wrong question

Read Matthew 19v1 – 6 aloud in the group (see below). Then answer the questions that follow.

> When Jesus had finished saying these things, he left Galilee and went into the region of Judea to the other side of the Jordan. Large crowds followed him, and he healed them there.
>
> Some Pharisees came to him to test him. They asked, "Is it lawful for a man to divorce his wife for any and every reason?"
>
> "Haven't you read," he replied, "that at the beginning the Creator 'made them male and female,' and said, 'For this reason a man will leave his father and mother and be united to his wife, and the two will become one flesh'? So

they are no longer two, but one flesh. Therefore what God has joined together, let no one separate.

1 As always, the Pharisees are trying to posture and corner Jesus with a challenging question. How does Jesus respond to their question about divorce?

2 Where does Jesus say marriage began? Why is this significant? Why does it matter?

Junk drawer theology

In love. What does that even mean?

"Love" is a junk drawer we dump all sorts of ideas into, just because we don't have anywhere else to put them.

I "love" God, and I "love" fish tacos. See the problem?

The way we use the word is so broad, so generic, that I'm not sure we understand it anymore. How should we define *love*?

(*Loveology*, p. 27)

 How do *you* define the word "love"?

How does *the world* define the word "love"?

5 What do people really mean when they say they have "fallen in love"?

6 How is love as a noun — an emotion — not a full picture of love? How do we know from the Scriptures that there is more to love than just emotion?

7 Describe the different words for "love" in Hebrew. How are they different from or similar to our modern view of love?

• *Rayah:*

• *Dod:*

• *Ahavah:*

Love incarnate

8 How does *God* define the word "love"? What context does he give us?

> This idea of Jesus as the model for how we are to love each other sounds docile and tame and cliché, but when we actually read about the life of Jesus, it's stunning.

(*Loveology,* p. 31)

Washing feet

There's a growing trend among followers of Jesus. During their wedding ceremony, the bride and groom take time to stop and wash each other's feet. In the moment, it's beautiful and emotive and romantic. The groom slips the bride's shoe off her foot. He gently dips her heel in the water, softly massages her foot while he rinses it with fresh water. He then dries it with a towel and puts her shoe back on her foot. The bride then does the same.

It's an amazing picture of service and love, but it's not quite there. You have to understand first-century culture to get the full picture of this practice.

Think dirt roads, hot temperatures, and high humidity. Think sandals, dust, livestock, and agriculture. Think manure and sand and sweat and stench.

In the first century, they didn't wash feet for symbolism. They washed feet out of sheer necessity. And it was a nasty job. One that was saved for the lowest of the low. The bottom of the barrel. Only servants. Only the lowest servants. It's hard to even compare the job to something equivalent today.

It is in this context that Jesus steps into this space. He gets on his knees, takes off his outer clothes, grabs a bowl, and gets to work. Scrubbing. Cleaning. Washing. The disciples didn't take this as a loving gesture. Read the story. They were outraged! It was wrong. Downright cruel. There was no way they were going to let their master — their rabbi — wash their filthy feet.

9 Read the story from John's perspective (John 13v1 – 17). What does this story tell us about love?

But the stories go on. The Scriptures are full of accounts that give us vivid pictures of Jesus' love for humanity. And seldom were they pleasant. One of the most graphic pictures of his love comes in John 19. The scourging. The Via Dolorosa. The cross. The death. All love. All grace. Life-changing if you can grasp the gravity and reality of it all.

10 Read about the Via Dolorosa (John 19v16–30). What does it tell us about love?

And then there's the original picture of love. The unadulterated plan. God's initial intent in all its innocence and beauty and grace. The Garden of Eden.

11 Read about the Garden of Eden (Genesis 2v18–25). What does it tell us about love?

12 Where in your life have you been misdefining love? How does Jesus' example change your outlook?

Scripture & prayer • 5 minutes

Choose two people to read the following Scripture aloud. Then individually meditate on its significance for your life, sharing your thoughts with the group if time permits. Challenge each other to memorize the verse during the coming week. End in prayer.

This is love: not that we loved God, but that he loved us, and sent his Son as an atoning sacrifice for our sins.

(1 John 4v10)

Midweek study: Love • 20 minutes

Based on the preface and chapter 1 of the Loveology *book*

Love: A word study

Is "love" a noun or verb? It makes a difference. What do the Scriptures teach us? Take some time during the week to see for yourself. Below are several passages that talk about love. Is it a *noun* (possessive; something you get; strong feelings), a *verb* (something that is done; something acted upon), or both?

- John 15v13 – Greater love has no one than this: to lay down one's life for one's friends.

- 1 Corinthians 13v4 – 7 – Love is patient, love is kind. It does not envy, it does not boast, it is not proud. It does not dishonor others, it is not self-seeking, it is not easily angered, it keeps no record of wrongs. Love does not delight in evil but rejoices with the truth. It always protects, always trusts, always hopes, always perseveres.

- Mark 12v30 – 31 – "'Love the Lord your God with all your heart and with all your soul and with all your mind and with all your strength.' The second is this: 'Love your neighbor as yourself.' There is no commandment greater than these."

- John 14v15 – If you love me, keep my commands.

- Genesis 29v20 – Jacob served seven years to get Rachel,

but they seemed like only a few days to him because of his love for her.

- 1 John 3v16 — This is how we know what love is: Jesus Christ laid down his life for us.

 Why does it make a difference if love is treated as a noun or verb? What are the implications?

 What does this tell us about God?

3 What does this tell us about marriage?

Session 2
Marriage

Based on chapters 2, 3, and 4 of the Loveology *book*

> I would argue that far too many of us have a decent idea what marriage is but are confused at best, if not clueless, as to what marriage is for.
>
> (*Loveology*, p. 45)

Introduction • 2 minutes

Most people throughout history get married because they are looking for happiness. They think it will be effortless and fun. They think their marriage—and their spouse—exists to bring them pure, unadulterated joy. You can imagine their surprise when things start to change—when their "strong feelings of emotion" begin to fade and reality sets in.

> At first, when my hand brushed up against my wife's, a light tingling feeling shot up my arm.
>
> Early on, when she would walk into the room, my pulse would speed up. I could feel the blood throbbing through my wrists. I was in college at the time, and staying focused in class was murder. My head was dizzy all the time.
>
> But a few years into our marriage, the electric feelings started to fade. My nervous system lost its hypersensitivity. My heart valve readjusted. The vertigo went away.
>
> It didn't take long to figure out that we were different people. Very different people. I'm introverted, type A, driven, and high-strung. She's über-social, laid-back, phlegmatic, and go with the flow. We started driving each other *crazy*.
>
> (*Loveology*, p. 43)

Dig in • 3 minutes

Before you watch the video, take time to dig into the following questions. Think about how they relate to you as an individual and then discuss them as a group.

Marriage is incredible, but it is far from bliss. It is one of the most amazing experiences as well as one of the most challenging. When two imperfect people come together with their own selfishness and self-reliance, you get more issues, more frustration, and more struggles. So what's the point of marriage? In your own words, why does marriage exist?

Video • 10 minutes

Play the Session 2 video. Take notes as you watch. What resonates with you? What concepts or thoughts are new to you? What do you agree with or disagree with?

Video notes

Marriage: The declining trend

What do we do when the feelings fade?

What is marriage for anyway?

The Genesis story and the first wedding

The first problem of creation — Adam is alone

Adam and Eve: A paradigm for all marriages

Friendship

Gardening

Sexuality

Family

Group discussion • 40 minutes

First impressions

Take a minute as a group to look over your notes and talk about a few things that hit you from the video. Share around the group.

1 What are some misperceptions we as a society have about marriage? What are some misperceptions you personally have about marriage? Be honest. Where have you gotten it wrong?

The first wedding

Read Genesis 2v15 – 25 aloud in the group (see below). Then answer the questions that follow.

> The LORD God took the man and put him in the Garden of Eden to work it and take care of it. And the LORD God commanded the man, "You are free to eat from any tree in the garden; but you must not eat from the tree of the knowledge of good and evil, for when you eat from it you will certainly die."
>
> The LORD God said, "It is not good for the man to be alone. I will make a helper suitable for him."
>
> Now the LORD God had formed out of the ground all the wild animals and all the birds in the sky. He brought them to the man to see what he would name them; and what-

ever the man called each living creature, that was its name. So the man gave names to all the livestock, the birds in the sky and all the wild animals.

But for Adam no suitable helper was found. So the LORD God caused the man to fall into a deep sleep; and while he was sleeping, he took one of the man's ribs and then closed up the place with flesh. Then the LORD God made a woman from the rib he had taken out of the man, and he brought her to the man.

The man said, "This is now bone of my bones and flesh of my flesh; she shall be called 'woman,' for she was taken out of man."

That is why a man leaves his father and mother and is united to his wife, and they become one flesh.

Adam and his wife were both naked, and they felt no shame.

2 What were the two biggest problems God saw with Adam's situation? Why did God declare that "it was not good"?

3 How do we know the story of Adam and Eve directly relates to each and every one of us today? Why are we convinced this marriage is a paradigm for all marriages? What points toward this conclusion in the Scriptures?

All you need is God

I cannot tell you how often I hear people say, "All you need is God." That makes for nice song lyrics, but the problem is, it's just not true. God never says, "All you need is God." Adam has God, and it's not enough. God says, "It is not good for the man to be alone"!

(*Loveology*, p. 52)

4 Why is it not good for man to be alone?

5 How does marriage give us a glimpse into the inner workings of God? How does marriage draw us closer to our Creator?

To know and be known

Your spouse is your closest friend.

That's one of the reasons God created marriage. For you to walk through life with the person you enjoy. With your spouse as the primary relationship in your life. Your *allup*. The one who knows you better than anybody. Better than your own mother.

To know and be known is a powerful thing. My wife knows all my flaws — trust me, there are many — and she *still* loves me. She still wants to get coffee and go for a walk. She still wants to spend her day off with me. This is one of my favorite things about my wife, hands down.

She's my friend.

(*Loveology*, p. 53)

6 Friendship is powerful. To know and be known. And no one should know you better than your spouse. How does this reality play out in marriage on a daily basis? How do you encourage closeness? How do you stifle it?

7 What areas are (or will be) the hardest areas of your life for you to share with your spouse? What has caused those barriers? Don't slide past this question. This is critical!

8 What does God mean in Genesis 1v28 when he says to Adam and Eve, "Be fruitful and increase in number; fill the earth and subdue it"?

Helper

9 God calls spouses to help each other "fill the earth and subdue it." But what does God mean when he calls us "helpers"?

10 This has become an explosive topic, especially among followers of Jesus. Where have we gotten the idea of "helper" wrong in the church?

11 Where have we gotten the idea of "helper" wrong in the world?

Redefining your expectations

12 Why do you want to get married? Or, why did you get married? Be honest. It's important to know what your expectations are.

13 Are those expectations for marriage reasonable, biblical, and God-honoring?

14 What needs to change within your thought process in order to have realistic expectations and goals for your marriage?

15 What should be your goals for marriage?

Scripture & prayer • 5 minutes

Choose two people to read the following Scripture aloud. Then individually meditate on its significance for your life, sharing your thoughts with the group if time permits. Challenge each other to memorize the verses during the coming week. End in prayer.

> Then God said, "Let us make mankind in our image, in our likeness, so that they may rule over the fish in the sea and the birds in the sky, over the livestock and all the wild animals, and over all the creatures that move along the ground."
>
> So God created mankind in his own image, in the image of God he created them; male and female he created them.
>
> (Genesis 1v26–27)

Midweek study: Marriage • 20 minutes

Based on chapters 2, 3, and 4 of the Loveology *book*

A theology of work

It may seem odd to talk about work when you think about marriage, but biblically, they are tightly connected — a symbiotic relationship melded together and feeding off one another. Read the following excerpt from the *Loveology* book and answer the questions that follow.

> The *first thing* God does with Adam is put him in the garden to "work it and take care of it."
>
> Everybody needs a gardening project.
>
> Put another way, everybody needs to find a calling in life. A sense of, "This is what I was put on earth to do. This is what I'm good at. This is what I was made for. This is my Eden, my corner of the earth to rule over."
>
> What's your calling? What's your gardening project? You need to be able to answer that question, or in time the wheels will fall off in your marriage. Why? Because *all healthy marriages are built around a calling.* Marriage is a means to an end. It exists for friendship, yes, but also to partner with God for the remaking of shalom.
>
> Couples who exist simply for one another are doomed to failure.

If the point of your marriage is *your marriage*, it will collapse in on itself.

If the end goal of your relationship is *your relationship*, it will self-destruct.

(*Loveology*, pp. 55 – 56)

We were created to rule over the world and subdue it — to actively partner with God, take the raw potentiality, and make something beautiful. We were made to work. But do you know your specific calling? Take some time to think about it.

Read Romans 12v1 – 8:

Therefore, I urge you, brothers and sisters, in view of God's mercy, to offer your bodies as a living sacrifice, holy and pleasing to God — this is your true and proper worship. Do not conform to the pattern of this world, but be transformed by the renewing of your mind. Then you will be able to test and approve what God's will is — his good, pleasing and perfect will.

For by the grace given me I say to every one of you: Do not think of yourself more highly than you ought, but rather think of yourself with sober judgment, in accordance with the faith God has distributed to each of you. For just as each of us has one body with many members, and these members do not all have the same function, so in Christ we, though many, form one body, and each member belongs to all the others. We have different gifts, according to the grace given to each of us. If your gift is prophesying, then prophesy in accordance with your faith; if it is serving, then serve; if it is teaching, then teach; if it is to encourage, then give encouragement; if it is giving, then give generously; if it is to lead, do it diligently; if it is to show mercy, do it cheerfully.

The thought process continues—if your gift is writing, or carpentry, or accounting, or parenting, or designing shoes, or serving coffee, do it diligently!

Your unique gifts

 What has God naturally gifted you to do? What are you good at? What skills have other people recognized in you?

2 How is God calling you to use your unique gifting to further his kingdom?

3 Maybe you are still figuring out your gifting. Maybe you are still trying to understand how God wired you. That is okay. But don't be afraid to dream. What interests has he given you? What passions are deep inside you? How do you see God using you in five, ten, or even twenty years?

A means to an end

4 Marriage is a means to an end. It exists to fulfill our calling from God. How can a spouse help you in your calling? How can he or she hurt you?

If you're married …

 What is your spouse's calling? How can you help your spouse accomplish his or her calling from God?

 What needs to change in your marriage in order for each of you to become more effective in your calling — to encourage, challenge, and support one another?

Session 3

Sex

Based on chapters 5, 6, and 7 of the Loveology *book*

We were made to worship God, but sin bends us in the direction of idolatry. We have a slant to take God's gifts and make them into wannabe gods.

Sex is no exception. In *Romans*, Paul writes, "God gave them over in the sinful desires of their hearts to sexual impurity for the degrading of their bodies with one another. They exchanged the truth about God for a lie, *and worshiped and served created things rather than the Creator.*"

(*Loveology*, p. 89)

Introduction • 2 minutes

How we think about sex has profound implications for marriage, dating, and life in general. Yet for many of us — if not all of us — our perspective has become warped and twisted, influenced by wrong theology and secular culture. The church often demonizes it while the world often idolizes it. Pornography degrades it. Selfishness confuses it. And dating entices it. So what is God's view on the subject of sex? You may be surprised.

> God saw *all* that he had made. Everything in the created order. The sand on the beach, and the sunset on the horizon. The sound of music. Food and drink. The human body. And everything we call "sex." Beauty, attraction, the desire of lovers, touch, arousal, foreplay, the joy of a kiss on your mouth, the orgasm — it's *all* good.
>
> In fact, sex is very good.
>
> What does this say about God? We have a tendency to think of God as austere and stoic. As if God's a grumpy old man who is mad at the world and doesn't want anybody to have fun. But nothing could be further from the truth.
>
> God is a God of pleasure.
>
> (*Loveology,* pp. 77–78)

Dig in • 3 minutes

Before you watch the video, take time to dig into the following questions. Think about how they relate to you as an individual and then discuss them as a group.

What were you taught about sex growing up? Was it viewed as negative and dirty, or beautiful and sacred? How has that influenced your own view of sex as an adult?

Video • 10 minutes

Play the Session 3 video. Take notes as you watch. What resonates with you? What concepts or thoughts are new to you? What do you disagree with?

Video notes

The progressive landslide

Sex and culture: How we think about sex

God's original intent ... it was very good

The first commandment in the Scriptures

Starting with the positive

We were sexual before we were sinful

Turning sex into a god

Echad: the power of sex

No such thing as casual sex

The beauty of a fresh start

Group discussion • 40 minutes

First impressions

Take a minute as a group to talk about a few things that hit you from the video. Refer to your notes and share around the group. This may be an uncomfortable topic, but it's vitally important. Be open and be respectful of others.

The great evil

If you've been part of a church for very long, you've probably heard plenty of messages on the topic of sex. Most likely, the vast majority of those messages cast sex in a negative light, providing a long list of "thou shall nots." Yet, that's not how God first approached the topic:

One of the first things we read about Adam and Eve is that they "were both naked, and they felt no shame." Can you imagine sex with no guilt or shame? Nothing to hide? Just pure, unadulterated joy between a man and a woman, locked into relationship for life. *That* is what God created.

And notice that all of this is before the fall. We were sexual *before* we were sinful. Sex is not an evil curse we have to curb and deny. It's a good gift we get to enjoy, as long as it's in the right context.

(*Loveology*, p. 81)

 How is God's view of sex different from *the church's view of sex?*

2 How is God's view of sex different from *your view of sex?*

3 If you are a woman, what are some lies you are being fed by culture that are distorting your view of sex? Where are you getting those lies? How can you protect yourself from those lies?

4 If you are a man, what are some lies you are being fed by culture that are distorting your view of sex? Where are you getting those lies? How can you protect yourself from those lies?

Echad

As you read the Scriptures, you'll see pretty quickly that God's perspective on sex is much higher than our own. And the word he uses over and over to describe sex is quite graphic. It's the Hebrew word *echad*. It is all of you—physical, emotional, and spiritual. The biblical picture is that of a fierce and permanent bond with another being. A bond so strong that if you try to rip it apart you cannot avoid real pain and anguish and suffering. Read what John Mark Comer has to say about *echad* in the book *Loveology*:

> *Echad* is when the lines blur between a man and a woman.
>
> *Echad* is when you're wrapped up so close with another human being that you're not really sure who's who anymore.
>
> *Echad* is when you know and are known.
>
> (*Loveology*, p. 96)

 How is *echad* different from the world's view of sex?

6 Why should *echad* be protected?

Sex, dating, and a messy past

There's no question we all bring baggage to marriage. Wrong thinking. Sinful pasts. Unhealthy tendencies. Abuse. What can we do to save ourselves from trouble? Think about the following questions and discuss them as a group.

 A lot of people talk about the dangers of physical ties in a dating relationship, but seldom does anyone warn about the emotional dangers of dating. What are some good boundaries or rules to help guard your heart emotionally in relationships before marriage?

8 What are some good boundaries for other relationships, even after marriage (with friends of the opposite sex, etc.)?

9 What sort of hope does a man or woman who has been sexually abused have for *echad* after experiencing such pain?

A God of forgiveness

This is a weighty topic. Far too many people have suffered the pain of *echad* outside God's original intent. They have taken God's gift and messed with it, misused it, or flat out disregarded his guidelines. But the good news is that he is a God of forgiveness. He is a God who heals.

> I don't know your story. Maybe your soul is bleeding right now. You've learned this truth the hard way. If only you could go back in time. If only you could have another chance. Then maybe, just maybe you could avoid the damage. Listen, here's the good news:
>
> Sex is powerful, but God is even more so. Do not underestimate what he can do in your life to put you back together. As a pastor, I get a front-row seat to watch the devastating effects of sin. But I also get to watch Jesus do his healing work. And I cannot tell you how many people I've seen renewed from the inside out after the tearing of *echad*.
>
> (*Loveology*, pp. 101 – 102)

10 Read 1 John 1v9 and Acts 3v19. What do the Scriptures say about forgiveness and restoration? Get specific. Can you find other passages as a group? How does this reality apply to someone who has ruined *echad*?

11 Read 1 Thessalonians 4v3–5 and 2 Timothy 2v22. What do the Scriptures say to persons who are enslaved in sexual sin right now? Maybe they are sleeping with their boyfriend or girlfriend. Messing around with porn. What hope is there for them? What actions should they take right now to find freedom and forgiveness?

Scripture & prayer • 5 minutes

Choose two people to read the following Scripture aloud. Then individually meditate on its significance for your life, sharing your thoughts with the group if time permits. Challenge each other to memorize the verses during the coming week. End in prayer.

> Do you not know that your bodies are temples of the Holy Spirit, who is in you, whom you have received from God? You are not your own; you were bought at a price. Therefore honor God with your bodies.
>
> (1 Corinthians 6v19 – 20)

Midweek study: Sex • 20 minutes

Based on chapters 5, 6, and 7 of the Loveology *book*

Sex and the lies we believe

> Somewhere along the way we forgot that God is after our joy.
>
> He's a lover, and you're the bride. He's a creator, and you're the creation. And to a greater degree than anyone else on the planet, God wants what's best for you. Especially when it comes to sex. *God wants you to have incredible sex.* The kind you dream about. The kind everybody is searching for. God wants that for you!
>
> And God, your maker and your lover, says that kind of sex is found in marriage. Guess what? He's right. Shocking, I know. Study after study shows that the people with the best sex lives are monogamous, heterosexual married couples who had few or no partners before marriage.
>
> (*Loveology,* p. 112)

Sex within marriage is amazing and euphoric. It brings you together. It draws you close. It provides healing and hope and love and peace. But it also takes work.

Many of us are believing a lie when it comes to marriage, life, love, and sex. As a woman, you are expecting Prince Charming to ride up and sweep you off your feet. Or as a man, you are expecting a gorgeous model to serve you and care for you and give you sex whenever you want. It doesn't quite work that way. (Sorry, guys.)

At its core, sex is a selfless act. A fun one, but selfless nonetheless. And for selfish people like us, that takes work.

If you're single ...

1 Is there anything you need to ask God's forgiveness for regarding sex in your past? What is it? Deal with it now!

2 What do you need to do right now to protect *echad* for yourself and your future spouse? How are you protecting yourself physically, emotionally, and spiritually?

3 Who do you know who can hold you accountable? Who can you go to with questions, concerns, or struggles?

If you're married ...

4 What do you need to do right now to better nourish *echad* with your spouse?

5 Do you think your spouse is satisfied with your sex life? If you're not sure, are you willing to ask him or her? And are you willing to make any changes he or she might suggest?

6 Are you satisfied with your sex life? If not, what do you need to discuss with your spouse?

Based on chapters 8, 9, and 10 of the Loveology *book*

> Love is a chase. A dance between a man and a woman.
> And it starts when a man says, "Come away," and the
> woman says, "Let us hurry ..."

(*Loveology,* p. 130)

Introduction • 2 minutes

What is it about us as humans that makes us captivated by romance? Think about it—one billion people tuned in to the royal wedding of Prince William and Kate Middleton in 2011. That's nearly 15 percent of the entire population of the planet!

And it's not just royal weddings. What movies are playing in the theaters right now? How many of them are romance stories or chick flicks? What about books? No doubt the bestsellers have to do with some lovesick vampire or a pair of star-crossed lovers. And what about magazines? What's hanging on the rack at the supermarket? How many of them focus on celebrity relationships or flings or childish gossip?

It's as if romance is hardwired into our DNA. This is what John Mark Comer has to say in the book *Loveology*:

> Maybe it's idealism. Maybe it's that we were raised on a steady diet of propaganda from Hollywood. Or maybe it's a dormant gene, something deep inside us, that scientists have yet to unearth. Maybe it's all of the above.
>
> But what's shocking to me is that when we actually get into a relationship and the fantasy becomes a reality, so often we're clueless about how to go forward. We're inundated with culture's dogmatic vision of what a relationship should (and shouldn't) look like, but we know it's a warped picture. The problem is, we just don't have a better one. It's like we're flying blind.
>
> (*Loveology*, p. 124)

Dig in • 3 minutes

Before you watch the video, take time to dig into the following questions. Think about how they relate to you as an individual and then discuss them as a group.

We're all captivated by romance. But do you know what it really should look like? In your own words, what do you think romance should look like premarriage? What should it look like in marriage?

Video • 10 minutes

Play the Session 4 video. Take notes as you watch. What resonates with you? What concepts or thoughts are new to you? What do you agree or disagree with?

Video notes

Hardwired for romance

Fantasy versus reality

God's example for a healthy relationship before marriage

The chase

The line

The friends

The journey to the day

The way of Jesus: A foundation well-built

Group discussion • 40 minutes

First impressions

Take a minute as a group to talk about a few things that hit you from the video. Share around the group.

The Song of Songs

Many would argue that the two greatest decisions you will ever make are (1) whether you will follow Jesus and (2) who you will marry. Yet, as a generation that is flying blind when it comes to romance and dating — desperately trying to filter the world's warped perspective along with our own — we need to take a serious look at the Scriptures to see what they say on the topic.

> In *The Song* we find four marks of a healthy relationship. By "relationship" I mean love, romance, and sexuality *before* marriage. Maybe you call that dating, or maybe you kissed dating good-bye and call it something else, or maybe you're from the East and your parents decide who you marry. Whatever the case, here are four marks of what your relationship should look like on the way to marriage.
>
> (*Loveology*, pp. 125 – 126)

1. The chase

"The chase" is the first mark of a healthy relationship. We as a culture spend a lot of time focused on "the chase." The pick-up lines. The hero scenarios. The perfect date — complete with flowers, dinner, and a movie. All the ways to "get the girl" and sweep her off her feet. But what does the chase really look like in the context of the Scriptures?

1 Read Song of Songs 2v8 – 13. What is the man's role in "the chase"?

2 Read Song of Songs 1v2 – 4. What is the woman's role in "the chase"?

2. The line

Go back to the Song of Songs, chapter 2, verses 6–7. Read it as a group.

> His left arm is under my head, and his right arm embraces me. Daughters of Jerusalem, I charge you by the gazelles and by the does of the field: Do not arouse or awaken love until it so desires.

 What is the Shulamite's challenge to those not yet married?

4 What is the Bible's answer to the question: "How far can we go before marriage?"

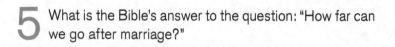

5 What is the Bible's answer to the question: "How far can we go after marriage?"

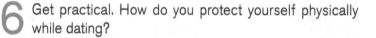

6 Get practical. How do you protect yourself physically while dating?

3. The friends

God doesn't want us to do life alone. That's why he made us relational beings. It's why he gave us friends and marriage and family (and social media).

7 What benefits do friends bring in the context of dating?

8 What should you specifically be asking of your friends regarding your dating relationships?

9 Do you have friends like that? Friends you can trust? Friends you can have real conversations with? If not, why? If yes, who are they? Lean in to them.

10 How do these friendships continue after marriage? What does that look like?

4. The journey to the day

11 What is the main point—the goal—of dating? Why do it at all?

12 How do you know when you are dating for the wrong reasons? What are some of those reasons?

But I have no one chasing me

There are a lot of amazing, frustrated women waiting to be chased. And a lot of guys waiting for the right woman to chase. So what do you do in the meantime?

13 How do you make the most of your non-dating time?

Scripture & prayer • 5 minutes

Choose two people to read the following Scripture aloud. Then individually meditate on its significance for your life, sharing your thoughts with the group if time permits. Challenge each other to memorize the verse during the coming week. End in prayer.

"For I know the plans I have for you," declares the LORD, "plans to prosper you and not to harm you, plans to give you hope and a future."

(Jeremiah 29v11)

Midweek study: Romance • 20 minutes

Based on chapters 8, 9, and 10 of the Loveology *book*

God's thoughts on romance

There is no question that God is a romantic. Just look at the Scriptures. The first picture we see—how God starts his epic narrative—is a love story. A wedding, of sorts. A beautiful garden. A man and a woman. A matchmaker—God. A union. A blessing. A commission—be fruitful and multiply. Classic. Clear. Romantic.

But it goes on.

The first miracle of Jesus takes place at a wedding (John 2). The first prayer request recorded in the Scriptures is a prayer for guidance in finding a spouse (Genesis 24). And it goes on from there. In fact, the final scene in the Scriptures is that of a wedding—between Jesus and his bride (Revelation 21). Fascinating.

Read what John Mark Comer has to say about it in the book *Loveology*:

> Now, I made it clear before that I think the idea of "the one" is a myth, and a dangerous one at that. There's no "soul mate" out there who will "complete you." I honestly believe my wife and I could have married any number of people and had a chance for a happy life, as long as our marriage was rooted in a love for one another and for God and formed around God's kingdom.

But ...

I also believe that God is a romantic. And we need to nuance this out a bit. There is no doubt in my mind that God brought Tammy and me together. Our story was scripted. And I don't think we're the outlier. I believe God's *involved* in your life to the degree that you open up your story to his authorship. In the beginning God brought Eve to Adam, and I think he's been doing that ever since.

I very much believe that God can and will lead you to your future spouse. And if you follow Jesus, I believe that God is shaping you for that day, just like I believe God is shaping me now for things that are twenty years in my future and nowhere on my radar. God's like that. *He's involved.*

(*Loveology,* p. 146)

Whether you are single or married, you have things you can work on. Spend the next few minutes answering the following questions.

1 Are you letting God — the great romantic — orchestrate your story, or are you controlling it yourself out of fear or insecurity or impatience?

What are your fears when it comes to marriage?

 What are your insecurities regarding your future or current spouse?

4 So much of the future depends on your present. How you are living right now matters. What can you do today to deal with your fears, insecurities, and impatience?

Session 5

Singleness

Based on chapter 13 of the Loveology *book*

For followers of Jesus, the point of singleness isn't freedom from responsibility. It's freedom *for more* responsibility.

(*Loveology*, p. 197)

Introduction • 2 minutes

In a world where marriage seems to be the definitive design, it can be awkward, or downright hell, for those who have yet to find a spouse. Or what about those who don't feel called to marriage at all? Or at least not yet? What do the Scriptures say to them?

Singleness is one of those blurry topics in the church. But it shouldn't be. It doesn't have to be. The Scriptures actually have a lot to say on the topic. In fact, there's an entire chapter in Paul's letter to the Corinthians that deals with it head on. (Read 1 Corinthians 7 when you have time.)

The one thing we must drill into our heads is this—life doesn't start when you get married. Life—true living—starts when you begin following Jesus. When you fold your story into the larger story of the kingdom of God.

That's a hard reality to grasp, especially in our modern culture. Especially within the church.

Dig in • 3 minutes

Before you watch the video, take time to dig into the following questions. Think about how they relate to you as an individual and then discuss them as a group.

How do you look at single people differently from married people? What is behind your thought process? What has led you to think that way?

Video • 10 minutes

Play the Session 5 video. Take notes as you watch. What resonates with you? What concepts or thoughts are new to you? What do you agree or disagree with?

Video notes

What the Scriptures say about singleness

Questions from the Corinthians

Following Jesus' example—should we get married at all?

Freedom for more responsibility

Following God's call

It's not a curse!

Life doesn't start when you get married

Waiting is a part of life

Jacob, Rachel, and Leah

The Lover is coming soon

Group discussion • 40 minutes

First impressions

Take a minute as a group to talk about a few things that hit
you from the video. Maybe this topic doesn't apply to you. Don't
check out. It applies to someone you know. Right thinking on
this subject is critically important if we are going to encourage
one another.

The gift nobody wants

As questions about marriage, sexuality, and divorce echo through culture, more and more people are choosing to go it alone. Whether we choose that path or it's given to us, we can't ignore the questions surrounding the topic of singleness.

Here's what John Mark Comer has to say in the book *Loveology*:

> The "gift of singleness" doesn't necessarily mean you don't want to get married. Scholars speculate that Paul was a widower. Maybe he missed married life. Maybe not. Either way, just because you have a calling and ability from God to live a single life doesn't mean you don't desire marriage.

> And it doesn't mean singleness is easy for you. It may be challenging. I have the gift of teaching. I believe it's what God put me on the planet to do. To be honest, it's the hardest thing I've ever done. It's labor. It's brutal at times. And more often than not, it's discouraging. However, there's something deep inside me that says, "I was made to do this."

(*Loveology*, p. 193)

1 How does someone know he or she was made to be single?

2 Is singleness a calling for a lifetime, or just a season? How do you know?

Matchmakers in the church

There is no question our culture looks down on single people. Especially within the church. Too often they are treated like the JV team — like they never really "made it."

3 How does a single person (who feels called to singleness) deal with the barrage of questions and dating setups?

How should we encourage those who are single without pushing our own agenda on them? Should we bring the matter up? Ignore it? Ask questions?

Your life and calling

For followers of Jesus, the point of singleness isn't freedom from responsibility. It's freedom *for more* responsibility. Paul thinks it's great if you stay single. At the end of the chapter he says he thinks it's "better" than marriage. But Paul isn't saying you should abdicate responsibility, work part-time, go surfing every day, travel a bit, play in a band that never goes anywhere, and do nothing but chill for ten years of your life. Does that sound anything like the gospel to you? To Paul, the point of singleness is to serve God in ways you can't if you're married.

(*Loveology,* pp. 197 – 198)

5 Spend some time as a group to give examples of calling or responsibility where it makes sense to be single. What does this look like for a man? What does this look like for a woman?

Waiting is a part of life

6 Some people are called to singleness for a time. How do you wait well? What does this look like?

7 How do we encourage others who are in this season?

Building the foundation

8 How you live right now matters. You are becoming your future *right now.* What do you need to work on right now to be ready for the life ahead? Think about it and then discuss it as a group.

Scripture & prayer • 5 minutes

Choose two people to read the following Scripture aloud. Then individually meditate on its significance for your life, sharing your thoughts with the group if time permits. Challenge each other to memorize the verse during the coming week. End in prayer.

> So do not fear, for I am with you; do not be dismayed, for I am your God. I will strengthen you and help you; I will uphold you with my righteous right hand.

> (Isaiah 41v10)

Midweek study: Singleness • 20 minutes

Based on chapter 13 of the Loveology *book*

Living in the letdown

Let's be honest. Life doesn't always go as planned. You have dreams. Expectations. Desires. Wants. Seldom do they *all* come to pass.

Look at the life of Jacob. He worked seven long years to get the girl of his dreams, only to be tricked into marrying her ugly sister Leah. A letdown, for sure. How do the Scriptures put it? "When morning came, there was Leah!" (Genesis 29v25). It might as well say, "In the morning, there was disappointment." Not at all what Jacob had hoped for.

> Life is full of letdowns. The human experience is anything but ideal.
>
> Whatever "it" is for you—college, graduation, a job, travel, an experience, success, fame, money, beauty—trust me, it's Leah. It can't live up to your expectations.
>
> (*Loveology*, p. 231)

How often do you wake up to disappointment? How many dreams have gone unfulfilled? It can really get you down. But look again at the Scriptures. What does God do with Jacob and Leah? He uses Leah (not Rachel, the wife Jacob really wanted) to usher in his kingdom through David, Solomon, Hezekiah, Josiah, and Jesus.

God works in the disappointments of life.

1 Where has Leah shown up in your life? What dreams have been crushed by unexpected reality? What areas of your life have left you questioning God? Is it a job, an experience, a relationship, success, fame, money, beauty?

2 Think through the letdowns you have had to deal with. Where have they left you? What have you learned? How has God used them?

3 What are you still holding on to that God is asking you to let go?

Live in the NOW

Life doesn't start when you get married. Or when you graduate or get a job or reach a goal — or whatever it is that you're waiting for. You're alive *now*. And life, as we all know, is evaporating. The biblical author James called it "a mist," like your breath on a February morning. Waiting for the Lord doesn't mean sitting around, working a dead-end job, watching TV, or hoping Mr. or Ms. Right falls into your lap. It means beginning to do good right where you're at, and then watching your story unfold.

(*Loveology*, pp. 160 – 161)

Insight for leaders

Thank you for taking your time and energy to lead a group through this study based on John Mark Comer's book *Loveology*. It is constructed around five sessions, including video teaching by John Mark and a time for group discussion. As a group leader, please do not feel the pressure to answer all the questions or reteach the material. Your role is simply to guide the process and manage the behind-the-scene details.

Make sure everyone in the group gets a copy of this study guide. Encourage them to use it to take notes, write down their thoughts, and process content. Remind them to bring it every time you gather. This will keep everyone on the same page and allow the time together to run efficiently.

Things to keep in mind as group leader:

- **Participation**—One of your key roles as group leader is to ensure everyone has the chance to participate and interact. Managing conversations can be hard. Do your best to make sure no one dominates the conversation and no one feels left out.

- **Safety**—Some of the topics covered in this five-week study will be very personal. It is your job as the group leader to set ground rules for the discussion. Make sure everyone agrees to keep conversations private and information confidential. Encourage the group to respect each other and where they are in life.

- **Prayer** — Start and end every gathering with prayer. You can ask someone else to do it, or you can do it yourself.

- **Hospitality** — Your most important job as a group leader is to ensure everyone feels welcome. Do whatever you can to create a comfortable environment for learning and sharing.

About the author

John Mark Comer is the pastor for teaching and vision at Bridgetown: A Jesus Church in Portland, Oregon. It's a city of coffee, food, culture, indie bands, and depressed people—he fits right in.

Prior to planting A Jesus Church in 2003, John Mark was the college pastor at a megachurch in Southern Oregon and played in a band. He is the author of *My Name Is Hope: Anxiety, Depression, and Life after Melancholy* and is wrapping up a master's degree in biblical and theological studies at Western Seminary.

John Mark lives in Portland with his wife, Tammy, their two boys, Jude and Moses, and their daughter, Sunday.

To sample more of John Mark's teachings on the Scriptures, Jesus, and life, go to ajesuschurch.org and sign up for the podcast.